# WOOD PELLET SMOKER GRILL COOKBOOK

## Delicious and Tasty Recipes to Become an Expert Barbecue Pitmaster with your Grill

*Adam Cook*

The information in the following pages is broadly considered a truthful and accurate account of facts and as such, any inattention, use, or misuse of the information in question by the reader will render any resulting actions solely under their purview. There are no scenarios in which the publisher or the original author of this work can be in any fashion deemed liable for any hardship or damages that may befall them after undertaking information described herein.

Additionally, the information in the following pages is intended only for informational purposes and should thus be thought of as universal. As befitting its nature, it is presented without assurance regarding its prolonged validity or interim quality. Trademarks that are mentioned are done without written consent and can in no way be considered an endorsement from the trademark holder.

# Summary

# Introduction

Barbecue has become very popular in the recent past, and many people have purchased their smoker grills. Smokers work by cooking meat over a wood fire, which gives the meat a special taste. That is why choosing the best one is essential. Wood Pellet Smoker Grills are the best because they are built with added features for high performance.

Wood pellet smoker grills are heating appliances that are made to cook mainly meat or fish, but also other dishes.

Normally, the food is cooked slowly over low heat. Most of the grills have a capacity of two hundred and sixty-eight degrees Fahrenheit. This heat, when combined with the meat, allows the food to smoke and cook. However, some wood pellet smoker grills can have as high as four hundred degrees Fahrenheit. When cooking with one of these grills, it is possible to sear steaks or cook brisket and ribs.

When choosing the best smoker grill, the material should be considered. Normally, most of the grills are made of cast iron. This is because it is non-porous, strong, and does not rust. However, the material of choice for cast iron is the alloy, which is known as Enameled Steel, manufactured by the Thermold Corporation. This material will not rust. Wood pellet smoker grills have several advantages:

1. No dirt disposal

When wood pellet smoker grills are in use, many parts are exposed to lots of dirt. This is why when the smoker is cleaned, a new layer of dirt may be formed. With smoke plated grills, this problem is solved. This is because the grills are placed in the smokers, and the smoke is circulated around the food and through the grills. This does not allow the dirt to build up, and the grills are kept clean. It also saves a lot of time since you will not have to clean them as often. For example, you will not have to clean the grills when smoking different foods like fish or chicken.

## 2. The ability to smoke and clean

After a little learning, most smokers and grills can be cleaned in the same process. The smoker has an open cover and the smoker bowl. When using the smoker, food is placed in the smoke, and everything is put together tightly. In this case, the smoker grills are well-insulated. This is mentioned in the manual of the smoker, and the smoker grills are built with tight covering. When grease is needed to cook, you will clean the grease tray and clean the smoker.

## 3. Large capacity

Most smokers have a large capacity. The size of the smoker does not dictate the size of the piece. You can use smoker grills for barbecuing many foods. The grills have a large burning surface to ensure that your meat is cooked properly and effectively.

## 4. Long Lasting

The materials the grills are made of are very durable. Most smokers are made of cast iron. The material is non-porous, so it does not rust and does not stain.

5. Easy to use

To use a smoker, there is a small learning curve. Many parts of the smoker are exposed, even when it is used inside the house. The smoker is prohibited in the location where it has been used in the past. Then, when using the smoker, burning wood is not necessary. You do not need to cut wood, fuel, and other heating materials. This is why wood pellet smoker grill is easy to use. It is very convenient, especially for people who have limited space.

6. Reliable

Another advantage of using a smoker grill is its reliability. Since there are many parts exposed in the smoker, the temperature of the food is easily monitored. The temperature of the food is also known from the length of time you decide to cook it. It is, therefore, an effective way for people who are unable to tend to the food while cooking.

Wood pellet smoker grills are useful because they are convenient. This is because wood pellets provide the same smoking action as a real pit but with a lot less work. Besides that, they do not take up too much space. You can even store it inside a closet when it is not in use. You will only need to keep it in an open space to use the smoker grill.

# 1. Grilled Shrimp Melody

Preparation Time: 30 minutes

Cooking time: 15 minutes

Servings: 4

Ingredients:

- ☐ 1 lb. potatoes
- ☐ 2 sliced ears of corn
- ☐ 6 tbsps. melted butter
- ☐ 8 oz. chicken breasts
- ☐ 1 lb. Shrimp
- ☐ 2 tbsps. fresh lemon juice
- ☐ 2 tsp. fresh thyme
- ☐ 2 minced garlic cloves
- ☐ 2 tsp. seafood seasoning
- ☐ 2 tbsps. chopped parsley

Directions:

1. Preheat the grill to a high temperature.

2. Arrange 8 pieces of aluminum foil.

3. Divide the potatoes, shrimp, chicken, and corn onto the sheets of foil.

4.　Using a medium bowl, mix the minced garlic, melted butter, chopped thyme, and lemon juice. Whisk together thoroughly.

5.　Pour the mixture over the shrimp mix and season with the seafood seasoning.

6.　Wrap the foil around the shrimp mix and arrange on the grill, cook for 15 minutes.

7.　Remove from the grill, garnish with the parsley and serve.

Nutrition:

Calories: 111

Fat: 6 g

Carbohydrates: 10 g

Protein: 13 g

# 2. Grilled Yellow Squash

Preparation Time: 30 minutes

Cooking time: 20 minutes

Servings: 8

Ingredients:

- ☐ 4 medium Yellow squash
- ☐ ½ c. extra virgin olive oil
- ☐ 2 crushed garlic cloves
- ☐ Salt
- ☐ pepper

Directions:

1. Preheat the grill for medium heat.

2. Using a medium pan, heat olive oil and add garlic cloves.

3. Cook over medium heat until the garlic becomes fragrant and sizzle.

4. Brush the slices of squash with garlic oil. Then season with salt and pepper.

5. Grill squash slices until they reach the desired tenderness, about 5 to 10 minutes per side. Occasionally turn and brush with additional garlic oil.

Nutrition:

Calories: 87

 Fat: 7 g

Carbohydrates: 6 g

Protein: 2 g

# 3.  Chicken Breast with Lemon

Preparation time: 15min

Cooking Time: 15min

Servings: 6

Ingredients:

- 6 Chicken breasts, skinless and boneless
- ½ cup Oil
- 1 - 2 Fresh thyme sprigs
- 1 tsp. ground black pepper
- 2 tsp. Salt
- 2 tsp. of Honey
- 1 Garlic clove, chopped
- 1 Lemon the juice and zest
- For service: Lemon wedges

Directions:

1.     Make the marinade: In a bowl combine the thyme, black pepper, salt, honey, garlic, and lemon zest and juice. Stir until dissolved and combined. Add in the oil and whisk to combine.

2.     Clean the breasts and pat dry. Place them in a plastic bag. Pour the pre-made marinade and

massage to distribute evenly. Place in the fridge, 4 hours.

3. Preheat the grill to 400F with the lid closed.

4. Drain the chicken and grill until the internal temperature reaches 165F, about 15 minutes.

5. Serve with lemon wedges and a side dish of your choice.

Nutrition:

Calories: 230

Proteins: 38g

Carbohydrates: 1g

Fat: 7g

# 4. Pellet Smoked Chicken Burgers

Preparation time: 20 minutes

Cooking time: 1 hour and 10 minutes

Servings: 6

Ingredients:

- 2 lb. ground chicken breast
- 2/3 cup of finely chopped onions
- 1 Tbsp. of cilantro, finely chopped
- 2 Tbsp. fresh parsley, finely chopped
- 2 Tbsp. of olive oil
- 1/2 tsp. of ground cumin
- 2 Tbsp. of lemon juice freshly squeezed
- 3/4 tsp. of salt and red pepper to taste

Directions:

1. In a bowl add all ingredients; mix until combined well.

2. Form the mixture into 6 patties.

3. Start your pellet grill on SMOKE (oak or apple pellets) with the lid open until the fire is established. Set the temperature to 350°F and preheat, lid closed, for 10 to 15 minutes.

4.    Smoke the chicken burgers for 45 - 50 minutes or until cooked through, turning every 15 minutes.

5.    Your burgers are ready when internal temperature reaches 165 °F.

6.    Serve hot.

Nutrition:

Calories: 221

Carbohydrates: 2.12g

Fat: 8.5g

 Fiber: 0.4g

Protein: 32.5g

# 5. Perfect Smoked Chicken Patties

Preparation time: 20 minutes

Cooking time: 50 minutes

Servings: 6

Ingredients:

- 2 lb. ground chicken breast
- 2/3 cup minced onion
- 1 Tbsp. cilantro (chopped)
- 2 Tbsp. fresh parsley, finely chopped
- 2 Tbsp. olive oil
- 1/8 tsp. crushed red pepper flakes, or to taste
- 1/2 tsp. ground cumin
- 2 Tbsp. fresh lemon juice
- 3/4 tsp. kosher salt
- 2 tsp. paprika
- Hamburger buns for serving

Directions:

1. In a bowl combine all ingredients from the list.

2.      Using your hands, mix well. Form mixture into 6 patties. Refrigerate until ready to grill (about 30 minutes).

3.      Start your pellet grill on SMOKE with the lid open until the fire is established). Set the temperature to 350°F and preheat, lid closed, for 10 to 15 minutes.

4.      Arrange chicken patties on the grill rack and cook for 35 to 40 minutes turning once.

5.      Serve hot with hamburger buns and your favorite condiments.

Nutrition:

Calories: 258

Carbohydrates: 2.5g

 Fat: 9.4g

Fiber: 0.6g

Protein: 39g

# 6. Grilled Chicken with Pineapple

Preparation Time: 1 hour

Cooking time: 1 hr. 15 minutes

Servings: 6

Ingredients:

- 2 lbs. Chicken tenders
- 1 c. sweet chili sauce
- ¼ c. fresh pineapple juice
- ¼ c. honey

Directions:

1. Combine the honey, pineapple juice, and sweet chili sauce in a medium bowl. Whisk together thoroughly.

2. Put ¼ cup of the mixture to one side.

3. Coat the chicken in the sauce.

4. Place a lid over the bowl and leave it in the fridge for 30 minutes to marinate.

5. Heat the grill to high heat.

6. Separate the chicken from the marinade and grill for 5 minutes on each side.

7. Use the reserved sauce to brush over the chicken.

8.    Continue to grill for a further 1 minute on each side.

9.    Take the chicken off the grill and let it rest for 5 minutes before servings.

Nutrition:

Calories: 270

 Fat: 2 g,

Carbohydrates: 25 g,

Protein: 33 g

# 7.    Smoked and Pulled Beef

Preparation Time: 10 minutes

Cooking Time: 6 hours

Servings: 6

Ingredients:

- 4 lb. beef sirloin tip roast
- 1/2 cup BBQ rub
- 2 bottles of amber beer
- 1 bottle barbecues sauce

Directions:

1.    Turn your wood pellet grill on smoke setting then trim excess fat from the steak.

2.    Coat the steak with BBQ rub and let it smoke on the grill for 1 hour.

3.    Continue cooking and flipping the steak for the next 3 hours. Transfer the steak to a braising vessel. Add the beers.

4.    Braise the beef until tender then transfer to a platter reserving 2 cups of cooking liquid.

5.    Use a pair of forks to shred the beef and return it to the pan. Add the reserved liquid and

barbecue sauce. Stir well and keep warm before serving.

6.     Enjoy.

Nutrition:

Calories 829

Total fat 46g

Saturated fat 18g

 Total carbs 4g

Net carbs 4g

Protein 86g

 Sugar 0g

Fiber 0g

Sodium: 181mg

# 8. Wood Pellet Smoked Beef Jerky

Preparation Time: 15 minutes

Cooking Time: 5 hours

Servings: 10

Ingredients:

- 3 lb. sirloin steaks, sliced into 1/4-inch thickness
- 2 cups soy sauce
- 1/2 cup brown sugar
- 1 cup pineapple juice
- 2 tbsp. sriracha
- 2 tbsp. red pepper flake
- 2 tbsp. hoisin
- 2 tbsp. onion powder
- 2 tbsp. rice wine vinegar
- 2 tbsp. garlic, minced

Directions:

1. Mix all the ingredients in a zip lock-bag. Seal the bag and mix until the beef is well coated. Ensure you get as much air as possible from the zip-lock bag.

2. Put the bag in the fridge overnight to let marinate. Remove the bag from the fridge 1 hour before cooking.

3. Start your wood pallet grill and set it to smoke. Layout the meat on the grill with half-inch space between them.

4. Let them cook for 5 hours while turning after every 2-1/2 hours.

5. Transfer from the grill and let cool for 30 minutes before serving.

6. Enjoy.

Nutrition:

Calories 80,

Total fat 1g,

Saturated fat 0g,

Total carbs 5g,

 Net carbs 5g,

Protein 14g,

Sugar 5g,

Fiber 0g,

Sodium: 650mg

# 9.  Reverse Seared Flank Steak

Preparation Time: 10 minutes

Cooking Time: 10 minutes

Servings: 2

Ingredients:

- 1.5 lb. Flanks steak
- 1 tbsp. salt
- 1/2 onion powder
- 1/4 tbsp. garlic powder
- 1/2 black pepper, coarsely ground

Directions:

1. Preheat your wood pellet grill to 225f

2. In a mixing bowl, mix salt, onion powder, garlic powder, and pepper. Generously rub the steak with the mixture.

3. Place the steaks on the preheated grill, close the lid, and let the steak cook.

4. Crank up the grill to high then let it heat. The steak should be off the grill and tented with foil to keep it warm.

5. Once the grill is heated up to 450°F, place the steak back and grill for 3 minutes per side.

6.    Remove from heat, pat with butter, and serve. Enjoy.

Nutrition:

Calories 112

Total fat 5g

Saturated fat 2g

Total carbs 1g

Net carbs 1g

Protein 16g

Sugar 0g

 Fiber 0g

Sodium: 737mg

# 10. Smoked Midnight Brisket

Preparation Time: 15 minutes

Cooking Time: 12 hours

Servings: 6

Ingredients:

- 1 tbsp. Worcestershire sauce
- 1 tbsp. beef Rub
- 1 tbsp. Chicken rub
- 1 tbsp. Blackened Saskatchewan rub
- 5 lb. flat cut brisket
- 1 cup beef broth

Directions:

1. Rub the sauce and rubs in a mixing bowl then rub the mixture on the meat.

2. Preheat your grill to 180°F with the lid closed for 15 minutes. You can use super smoke if you desire.

3. Place the meat on the grill and grill for 6 hours or until the internal temperature reaches 160°F.

4. Remove the meat from the grill and double wrap it with foil.

5.     Add beef broth and return to grill with the temperature increased to 225°F. Cook for 4 hours or until the internal temperature reaches 204°F.

6.     Remove from the grill and let rest for 30 minutes. Serve and enjoy with your favorite BBQ sauce.

Nutrition:

Calories 200

Total fat 14g

Saturated fat 6g

Total carbs 3g

 Net carbs 3g

Protein 14g

Sugar 0g

Fiber 0g

Sodium: 680mg

# 11. Grilled Butter Basted Porterhouse Steak

Preparation Time: 10 minutes

Cooking Time: 40 minutes

Servings: 4

Ingredients:

- 4 tbsp. butter, melted
- 2 tbsp. Worcestershire sauce
- 2 tbsp. Dijon mustard
- Prime rib rub

Directions:

1. Set your wood pellet grill to 225°F with the lid closed for 15 minutes.

2. In a mixing bowl, mix butter, sauce, Dijon mustard until smooth. Brush the mixture on the meat then season with the rub.

3. Arrange the meat on the grill grate and cook for 30 minutes.

4. Use tongs to transfer the meat to a pattern then increase the heat to high.

5. Return the meat to the grill grate to grill until your desired doneness is achieved.

6.    Baste with the butter mixture again if you desire and let rest for 3 minutes before serving. Enjoy.

Nutrition:

Calories 726

Total fat 62g

Saturated fat 37g

Total carbs 5g

 Net carbs 4g

Protein 36g

 Sugar 1g

Fiber 1g

Sodium: 97mg

Potassium 608mg

# 12. Cocoa Crusted Grilled Flank steak

Preparation Time: 10 minutes

Cooking Time: 6 minutes

Servings: 6

Ingredients:

- ☐ 1 tbsp. cocoa powder
- ☐ 2 tbsp. chili powder
- ☐ 1 tbsp. chipotle chili powder
- ☐ 1/2 tbsp. garlic powder
- ☐ 1/2 tbsp. onion powder
- ☐ 1-1/2 tbsp. brown sugar
- ☐ 1 tbsp. cumin
- ☐ 1 tbsp. smoked paprika
- ☐ 1 tbsp. kosher salt
- ☐ 1/2 tbsp. black pepper
- ☐ Olive oil
- ☐ 4 lb. Flank steak

Directions:

1. Whisk together cocoa, chili powder, garlic powder, onion powder, sugar, cumin, paprika, salt, and pepper in a mixing bowl.

2.     Drizzle the steak with oil then rub with the cocoa mixture on both sides.

3.     Preheat your wood pellet grill for 15 minutes with the lid closed.

4.     Cook the meat on the grill grate for 5 minutes or until the internal temperature reaches 135°F.

5.     Remove the meat from the grill and let it cool for 15 minutes to allow the juices to redistribute.

6.     Slice the meat against the grain and on a sharp diagonal.

7.     Serve and enjoy.

Nutrition:

Calories 420

Total fat 26g

Saturated fat 8g

Total carbs 21g

Net carbs 13g

 Protein 3g

Sugar 7g

 Fiber 8g

Sodium: 2410mg

# 13. Wood Pellet Grill Prime Rib Roast

Preparation Time: 10 minutes

Cooking Time: 4 hours

Servings: 10

Ingredients:

- 7 lb. bone prime rib roast
- prime rib rub

Directions:

1. Coat the roast generously with the rub then wrap in a plastic wrap. Let sit in the fridge for 24 hours to marinate.

2. Set the temperatures to 500°F.to to preheat with the lid closed for 15 minutes.

3. Place the rib directly on the grill fat side up and cook for 30 minutes.

4. Reduce the temperature to 300°F and cook for 4 hours or until the internal temperature is 120°F-rare, 130°F-medium rare, 140°F-medium, and 150°F-well done.

5. Remove from the grill and let rest for 30 minutes then serve and enjoy.

Nutrition:

Calories 290

Total fat 23g

Saturated fat 9.3g

Protein 19g

Sodium: 54mg

Potassium 275mg

# 14. Smoked Longhorn Cowboy Tri-Tip

Preparation Time: 10 minutes

Cooking Time: 4 hours

Servings: 7

Ingredients:

☐     3 lb. tri-tip roast 1/8 cup coffee, ground

☐     1/4 cup beef rub

Directions:

1.     Preheat the grill to 180°F with the lid closed for 15 minutes. Meanwhile, rub the roast with coffee and beef rub. Place the roast on the grill grate and smoke for 3 hours. Remove the roast from the grill and double wrap it with foil. Increase the temperature to 275°F. Return the meat to the grill and let cook for 90 minutes or until the internal temperature reaches 135°F.

2.     Remove from the grill, unwrap it and let rest for 10 minutes before serving.

Nutrition:

Calories 245

 Total fat 14g

Saturated fat 4g

Protein 23g

Sodium: 80mg

# 15. Wood Pellet Grill Teriyaki Beef Jerky

Preparation Time: 10 minutes

Cooking Time: 5 hours

Servings: 6

Ingredients:

- 3 cups soy sauce
- 2 cups brown sugar
- 3 garlic cloves
- 2-inch ginger knob, peeled and chopped
- 1 tbsp. sesame oil
- 4 lb. beef, skirt steak

Directions:

1. Place all the ingredients except the meat in a food processor. Pulse until well mixed.

2. Trim any excess fat from the meat and slice into 1/4-inch slices. Add the steak with the marinade into a zip lock bag and let marinate for 12-24 hours in a fridge.

3. Set the wood pellet grill to smoke and let preheat for 5 minutes.

4.     Arrange the steaks on the grill leaving a space between each. Let smoke for 5 hours.

5.     Remove the steak from the grill and serve when warm.

Nutrition:

Calories 80

Total fat 1g

Saturated fat 0g

Total Carbs 7g

Net Carbs 0g

Protein 11g

Sugar 6g

Fiber 0g

Sodium: 390mg

# 16. Grilled Butter Basted Rib-eye

Preparation Time: 20 minutes

Cooking Time: 25 minutes

Servings: 4

Ingredients:

- ☐ 2 rib-eye steaks, bone-in
- ☐ Salt to taste
- ☐ Pepper to taste
- ☐ 4 tbsp. butter, unsalted

Directions:

1. Mix steak, salt, and pepper in a zip-lock bag. Seal the bag and mix until the beef is well coated. Ensure you get as much air as possible from the zip-lock bag.

2. Set the wood pellet grill temperature to high with the lid closed for 15 minutes. Place a cast-iron into the grill.

3. Place the steaks on the hottest spot of the grill and cook for 5 minutes with the lid closed.

4. Open the lid and add butter to the skillet. When it's almost melted place the steak on the skillet with the grilled side up.

5.   Cook for 5 minutes while busting the meat with butter. Close the lid and cook until the internal temperature is 130°F.

6.   Remove the steak from the skillet and let rest for 10 minutes before enjoying with the reserved butter.

Nutrition:

Calories 745

Total fat 65g

Saturated fat 32g

 Total Carbs 5g

 Net Carbs 5g

 Protein 35g

# 17. Wood Pellet Smoked Brisket

Preparation Time: 20 minutes

Cooking Time: 9 hours

Servings: 10

Ingredients:

- 2 tbsp. garlic powder
- 2 tbsp. onion powder
- 2 tbsp. paprika
- 2 tbsp. chili powder
- 1/3 cup salt
- 1/3 cup black pepper
- 12 lb. whole packer brisket, trimmed
- 1-1/2 cup beef broth

Directions:

1. Set your wood pellet temperature to 225°F. Let preheat for 15 minutes with the lid closed.

2. Meanwhile, mix garlic, onion, paprika, chili, salt, and pepper in a mixing bowl.

3. Season the brisket generously on all sides.

4. Place the meat on the grill with the fat side down and let it cool until the internal temperature reaches 160°F. Remove the meat from the grill

and double wrap it with foil. Return it to the grill and cook until the internal temperature reaches 204°F.

5.     Remove from the grill, unwrap the brisket, and let sit for 15 minutes.

6.     Slice and serve.

Nutrition:

Calories 270

Total fat 20g

Saturated fat 8g

Total Carbs 3g

Net Carbs 3g

Protein 20g

Sugar 1g

Fiber 0g

Sodium: 1220mg

# 18. Beef Jerky

Preparation Time: 15 minutes

Cooking Time: 5 hours

Servings: 10

Ingredients:

- ☐ 3 lb. sirloin steaks
- ☐ 2 cups soy sauce
- ☐ 1 cup pineapple juice
- ☐ 1/2 cup brown sugar
- ☐ 2 tbsp. sriracha
- ☐ 2 tbsp. hoisin
- ☐ 2 tbsp. red pepper flake
- ☐ 2 tbsp. rice wine vinegar
- ☐ 2 tbsp. onion powder

Directions:

1. Mix the marinade in a zip lock bag and add the beef. Mix until well coated and remove as much air as possible.

2. Place the bag in a fridge and let marinate overnight or for 6 hours. Remove the bag from the fridge an hour before cooking 3) Startup the

wood pellet and set it on the smoking settings or at 1900F.

3.     Lay the meat on the grill leaving a half-inch space between the pieces. Let cool for 5 hours and turn after 2 hours.

4.     Remove from the grill and let cool. Serve or refrigerate

Nutrition:

Calories 309

Total fat 7g

Saturated fat 3g

 Total carbs 20g

Net carbs 19g

Protein 34g

Sugars 15g

 Fiber 1g

Sodium 2832mg

# 19. Smoked Beef Roast

Preparation Time: 10 minutes

Cooking Time: 6 hours

Servings: 6

Ingredients:

- 1-3/4 lb. beef sirloin tip roast
- 1/2 cup BBQ rub
- 2 bottles of amber beer
- 1 bottle BBQ sauce

Directions:

1. Turn the onto the smoke setting.

2. Transfer the beef to a pan and add the beer. The beef should be 1/2 way covered.

3. Braise the beef until fork tender. It will take 3 hours on the stovetop and 60 minutes on the instant pot.

4. Remove the beef from the ban and reserve 1 cup of the cooking liquid.

5. Use 2 forks to shred the beef into small pieces then return to the pan with the reserved braising liquid.

6.    Add BBQ sauce and stir well then keep warm until serving. You can also reheat if it gets cold.

Nutrition:

Calories 829,

Total fat 46g,

Saturated fat 18g,

Total carbs 4g,

Net carbs 4g

 Protein 86g,

Sugars 0g,

 Fiber 0g,

Sodium 181mmg

# 20. Beef Tenderloin

Preparation Time: 10 minutes

Cooking Time: 45 minutes

Servings: 6

Ingredients:

- 4 lb. beef tenderloin
- 3 tbsp. steak rub
- 1 tbsp. kosher salt

Directions:

1. Preheat to high heat. Meanwhile, trim excess fat from the beef and cut it into 3 pieces. Coat the steak with rub and kosher salt. Place it on the grill. Close the lid and cook for 10 minutes. Open the lid, flip the beef and cook for 10 more minutes. Reduce the temperature of the grill to 2250F and smoke the beef until the internal temperature reaches 1300F.

2. Remove the beef from the grill and let rest for 15 minutes before slicing and serving.

Nutrition:

Calories 999

Total fat 76g

Saturated fat 30g

Protein 74g

Sodium 1234mmg

# 21. New York Strip

Preparation Time: 5 minutes

Cooking Time: 15 minutes

Servings: 6

Ingredients:

☐     3 New York strips

☐     Salt and pepper

Directions:

1.     If the steak is in the fridge, remove it 30 minutes before cooking.

2.     Preheat the to 4500F.

3.     Meanwhile, season the steak generously with salt and pepper. Place it on the grill and let it cook for 5 minutes per side or until the internal temperature reaches 1280F.

4.     Remove the steak from the grill and let it rest for 10 minutes.

Nutrition:

Calories 198

Total fat 14g     Saturated fat 6g

Protein 17g     Sodium 115mg

# 22. Stuffed Peppers

Preparation Time: 20 minutes

Cooking Time: 5 minutes

Servings: 6

Ingredients:

- 3 bell peppers, sliced in halves
- 1 lb. ground beef, lean
- 1 onion, chopped
- 1/2 tbsp. red pepper flakes
- 1/2 tbsp. salt
- 1/4 tbsp. pepper
- 1/2 tbsp. garlic powder
- 1/2 tbsp. onion powder
- 1/2 cup white rice
- 15 oz. stewed tomatoes
- 8 oz. tomato sauce
- 6 cups cabbage, shredded
- 1-1/2 cup water
- 2 cups cheddar cheese

Directions:

1. Arrange the pepper halves on a baking tray and set aside.

2.     Preheat your grill to 3250F.

3.     Brown the meat in a large skillet. Add onions, pepper flakes, salt, pepper garlic, and onion and cook until the meat is well cooked.

4.     Add rice, stewed tomatoes, tomato sauce, cabbage, and water.

5.     Cover and simmer until the rice is well cooked, the cabbage is tender and there is no water in the rice.

6.     Place the cooked beef mixture in the pepper halves and top with cheese.

7.     Place in the grill and cook for 30 minutes.

8.     Serve immediately and enjoy it.

Nutrition:

Calories 422

Total fat 22g     Saturated fat 11g

Total carbs 24g     Net carbs 19g

Protein 34g     Sugars 11g

Fiber 5g     Sodium 855mg

# 23. Prime Rib Roast

Preparation Time: 10 minutes

Cooking Time: 2 hours

Servings: 8

Ingredients:

- 5 lb. rib roast, boneless
- 4 tbsp. salt
- 1 tbsp. black pepper
- 1-1/2 tbsp. onion powder
- 1 tbsp. granulated garlic
- 1 tbsp. rosemary
- 1 cup chopped onion
- 1/2 cup carrots, chopped
- 1/2 cup celery, chopped
- 2 cups beef broth

Directions:

1. Remove the beef from the fridge 1 hour before cooking.

2. Preheat the Wood Pellet to 2500F.

3. In a small mixing bowl, mix salt, pepper, onion, garlic, and rosemary to create your rub.

4.    Generously coat the roast with the rub and set it aside.

5.    Combine chopped onions, carrots, and celery in a cake pan then place the bee on top.

6.    Place the cake pan in the middle of the and cook for 1 hour.

7.    Pour the beef broth at the bottom of the cake pan and cook until the internal temperature reaches 1200F.

8.    Remove the cake pan from the and let rest for 20 minutes before slicing the meat.

9.    Pour the cooking juice through a strainer, and then skim off any fat at the top.

10.   Serve the roast with the cooking juices.

Nutrition:

Calories 721

Total fat 60g      Saturated fat 18g

Total carbs 3g      Net carbs 2g

Protein 43g      Sugars 1g

Fiber 1g      Sodium 2450mmg

# 24. Fine Indian Smoked T-Bone

Preparation Time: 20 minutes

Cooking Time: 45 minutes

Servings: 12

Ingredients:

☐ 1-pound beef tenderloin, cut into 1-inch cubes

☐ 2 pounds strip steak, cut into 1-inch cubes

☐ 1 large onion, cut into 1-inch cubes

☐ 1 bell pepper, cut into 1-inch cubes

☐ 1 zucchini, cut into 1-inch cubes

☐ 10 ounces cherry tomatoes

☐ ¼ cup olive oil

☐ ½ cup steak seasoning

Directions:

1. Take a large bowl and add tenderloin, strip steak, onion, zucchini, bell pepper, tomatoes and mix well with olive oil

2. Season with steak seasoning and stir until the meat has been coated well

3. Cover the meat and allow it to refrigerate for 4-8 hours

4.    Preheat your smoker to 225 degrees Fahrenheit using your desired wood

5.    Make the kebabs by skewering meat and veggies Alternatively make sure, to begin with, meat and end with meat Transfer the skewers to your smoker rack and smoke for 45 minutes

6.    Remove once the internal temperature reaches 135 degrees Fahrenheit (for a RARE finish)

7.    Serve and enjoy!

Nutrition:

Calories: 559

Fats: 5g

Carbs: 57g

Fiber: 1g

# 25. The South Barbacoa

Preparation Time: 15 minutes

Cooking Time: 3 hours

Servings: 10

Ingredients:

- ☐ 1 and ½ teaspoon pepper
- ☐ 1 tablespoon dried oregano
- ☐ 1 and ½ teaspoon cayenne pepper
- ☐ 1 and ½ teaspoon chili powder
- ☐ 1 and ½ teaspoon garlic powder
- ☐ 1 teaspoon ground cumin
- ☐ 1 teaspoon salt
- ☐ 3 pounds boneless beef chuck roast

Directions:

1.  Add dampened hickory wood to your smoker and preheat to 200 degrees Fahrenheit

2.  Take a small bowl and add oregano, cayenne pepper, black pepper, garlic powder, chili powder, cumin, salt, and seasoned salt

3.  Mix well

4.  Dip the chuck roast into your mixing bowl and rub the spice mix all over

5.    Transfer the meat to your smoker and smoker for 1 and a ½ hours

6.    Make sure to turn the meat after every 30 minutes, if you see less smoke formation, add more Pellets after every 30 minutes as well

7.    Once the meat shows a dark red color with darkened edges, transfer the meat to a roasting pan and seal it tightly with an aluminum foil

8.    Preheat your oven to 325 degrees Fahrenheit

9.    Transfer the meat to your oven and bake for 1 and a ½ hours more

10.   Shred the meat using two forks and serve!

Nutrition:

Calories: 559

Fats: 5g

Carbs: 57g

Fiber: 1g

# 26. Smoked Pork Ribs Black Pepper

Preparation time: 30 minutes

Cooking Time: 6 Hours

Servings: 1

Ingredients:

- Pork Baby Back Ribs (6-lbs., 2.7-kgs)
- Salt – ½ cup
- Black pepper – ¾ cup
- Sweet smoked paprika – 1 tablespoon
- Sugar – 3 tablespoons
- Mustard powder – 1 tablespoon

Directions:

1. Combine salt with black pepper, sweet smoked paprika, sugar, and mustard powder. Stir until mixed.

2. Rub the pork baby ribs with the salt mixture then place in disposable aluminum pan. Set aside.

3. Preheat the smoker to 225°F (107°C) with charcoal and peach wood chips then wait until it reaches the desired temperature.

4.     Once the smoker is ready, place the disposable aluminum pan in the smoker.

5.     Smoke the pork baby ribs for 6 hours or until the internal temperature has reached 205°F (96°C).

6.     Remove the smoked pork ribs from the smoker then transfer to a serving dish.

7.     Serve and enjoy.

Nutrition:

Carbohydrates: 4g

Protein: 86 g

Fat: 46 g

Sodium: 181 mg

Cholesterol: 295 mg

# 27. Smoked Brown Pork Butt with Apple Injection

Preparation time: 30 minutes

Cooking Time: 6 Hours

Servings: 10

Ingredients:

- Pork Butt (6-lbs., 2.7-kgs)
- The Liquid Injection
- Chicken stock – 1 ¼ cups
- Apple juice – 1 ½ cups
- Apple cider vinegar – 3 tablespoons
- Barbecue sauce – 3 tablespoons
- Worcestershire sauce – 1 ½ tablespoons
- The Rub
- Brown sugar – 3 tablespoons
- Salt – 3 tablespoons
- Smoked paprika – 2 tablespoons
- Onion powder – 2 ¼ tablespoons
- Garlic powder – 2 tablespoons
- Oregano – ¾ tablespoon
- Cumin – ¾ teaspoon
- Black pepper – ¾ teaspoon

Directions:

1.    Pour chicken broth into a saucepan then add apple juice, apple cider vinegar, barbecue sauce, and Worcestershire sauce into the saucepan.

2.    Bring to a simmer and stir until incorporated.

3.    Remove from heat and let it cool for approximately 30 minutes. Set aside.

4.    Combine the rub ingredients then mix well.

5.    Preheat the smoker to 225°F (107°C) with charcoal and peach wood chips. Use the indirect heat.

6.    While waiting for the smoker, inject the pork butt with the liquid injection then coat the pork butt with the rub mixture.

7.    Once the smoker has reached the desired temperature, place the seasoned pork butt in the smoker.

8.    Smoke the pork butt for 12 hours and check the smoke once every hour. Add more soaked peach wood chips if it is necessary.

9.    When the pork butt is ready or the internal temperature has reached 205°F (96°C), remove the smoked pork butt from the smoker then transfer to a serving dish.

10.    Let the smoked pork butt cool for a few minutes then chop or pull the pork.

11.    Serve and enjoy.

Nutrition:

Carbohydrates: 4g

Protein: 86 g

Fat: 46 g

Sodium: 181 mg

Cholesterol: 295 mg

# 28. Refreshing Smoked Pork Tenderloin with Orange Glaze

Preparation time: 30 minutes

Cooking Time: 6 Hours

Servings: 10

Ingredients:

- Pork Tenderloin (6-lbs., 2.7-kgs)
- The Glaze
- Unsweetened orange juice – 1 ½ cups
- Sugar – 1 cup
- Olive oil – 1 ¼ cups

Directions:

1. Preheat the smoker to 225°F (107°C) with charcoal and peach wood chips. Use the indirect heat.

2. Pour orange juice into a saucepan then bring to boil.

3. Once it is boiled, stir in sugar and stir until the sugar is completely dissolved.

4. When the mixture is incorporated, remove from heat then let it cool for a few minutes.

5. After that, stir in olive oil then mix well.

6. Place the pork loin in a disposable aluminum pan then drizzle the orange juice mixture over the pork.

7. Once the smoker has reached the desired temperature, place the pan in the smoker.

8. Smoke the pork tenderloin for about 6 hours or until the internal temperature has reached 145°F (63°C).

9. When it is done, remove the pan from the smoker and transfer to a serving dish together with the liquid.

10. Cut the pork tenderloin into thick slices then serve.

11. Enjoy!

Nutrition:

Carbohydrates: 4g

Protein: 86 g

Fat: 46 g

Sodium: 181 mg

Cholesterol: 295 mg

# 29. Simple Smoked Garlic Pork Chop

Preparation time: 30 minutes

Cooking Time: 6 Hours

Servings: 10

Ingredients:

- Pork Chops (6-lbs., 2.7-kgs)
- Olive oil – ¼ cup
- The Rub
- Salt – ¼ cup
- Pepper – 2 tablespoons
- Garlic powder – 2 tablespoons
- Minced garlic – 2 tablespoons

Directions:

1.     Preheat the smoker to 250°F (121°C) with charcoal and hickory wood chips. Use the indirect heat.

2.     Rub the pork chops with salt, pepper, garlic powder, and minced garlic. Set aside.

3.     Preheat a skillet over medium heat then pour olive oil into the skillet.

4.    Once the olive oil is hot, stir in the seasoned pork chops then sauté until just wilted.

5.    Transfer the sautéed pork chops to a disposable aluminum pan then place in the smoker.

6.    Smoke the pork chops for 5 hours and check the smoke regularly. Add more soaked hickory wood chips if it is necessary.

7.    Once the internal temperature has reached 145°F (63°C), take the smoked pork chops from the smoker.

8.    Transfer the smoked pork chops to a serving dish and serve with any kinds of fruit and vegetable, as you desired.

9.    Enjoy.

Nutrition:

Carbohydrates: 4g

Protein: 86 g

Fat: 46 g

Sodium: 181 mg

Cholesterol: 295 mg

# 30. Smoked Pork Shoulder with Herbs

Preparation time: 15 minutes

Cooking Time: 6 Hours

Servings: 1

Ingredients:

- Boneless Pork Shoulder (6-lbs., 2.7-kgs)
- The Rub
- Salt – 2 tablespoons
- Turmeric – 1 ½ tablespoons
- Cumin – ¾ tablespoon
- Coriander – ¾ tablespoon
- Sugar – ½ tablespoon
- Cardamom – 1 teaspoon

Directions:

- Preheat the smoker to 250°F (121°C) with charcoal and hickory wood chips. Use the indirect heat.
- Place salt, turmeric, cumin, coriander, sugar, and cardamom in a bowl then mix well.
- Rub the pork shoulder with the spice mixture then place in a disposable aluminum pan.

☐ Place the pan in the smoker then smoke the pork shoulder for 6 hours. Add more charcoal and wood chips if it is needed.

☐ Check the smoked pork shoulder and when the internal temperature has reached 145°F (63°C), take the smoked pork chops from the smoker.

☐ Place the smoked pork shoulder on a flat surface then let it cool for a few minutes.

☐ Shred the smoked pork shoulder then transfer to a serving dish.

☐ Serve and enjoy.

Nutrition:

Carbohydrates: 4g

Protein: 46 g

Fat: 16 g

Sodium: 28 mg

Cholesterol: 95 mg

# 31. Sweet Smoked Rabbit Honey

Preparation time: 30 minutes

Cooking Time: 12 Hours

Servings: 10

Ingredients:

- Rabbits 2 (6-lbs., 2.7-kgs)
- The Rub
- Minced garlic – 3 tablespoons
- Garlic powder – 2 tablespoons
- Lemon juice – 3 tablespoons
- Salt – 2 tablespoons
- Pepper – 2 ½ tablespoons
- The Glaze
- Honey – ¼ cup
- Olive oil – 2 tablespoons

Directions:

1. Rub the rabbits with minced garlic; garlic powder, lemon juice, salt, and pepper then cover with plastic wrap.

2. Refrigerate the seasoned rabbits for about 8 hours until the spice is completely absorbed to the rabbits.

3. Preheat a smoker to 225°F (107°C) with charcoal and hickory wood chips.

4. When the smoker is ready, unwrap the rabbits then place in the smoker.

5. Smoke the rabbits for 3 hours and check once every hour. Add more charcoal and wood chips to keep the smoke.

6. After 3 hours, remove the rabbits from the smoker then brush with olive oil and honey mixture.

7. Place the glazed rabbits in a disposable aluminum pan then return back to the smoker.

8. Smoke the rabbits for another 3 hours then brush with remaining honey and olive oil mixture once every hour.

9. When the smoked rabbits are done, remove from the smoker and transfer to a serving dish.

10. Cut the rabbits into pieces then serve.

11. Enjoy!

Nutrition:

Carbohydrates: 4g

Protein: 46 g

Fat: 16 g

Sodium: 28 mg

Cholesterol: 95 mg

# 32. Smoked Rabbit with Dry Rub

Preparation time: 30 minutes

Cooking Time: 7 Hours

Servings: 5

Ingredients:

- Rabbits 2 (6-lbs., 2.7-kgs)
- The Rub
- Paprika – 1 cup
- Cayenne pepper – ¼ cup
- Black pepper – ½ cup
- Garlic powder – ¾ cup
- Onion powder – ¼ cup
- Salt – ½ cup
- Dried oregano – ¼ cup
- Thyme – ¼ cup

Directions:

1. Combine all of the dry rub ingredients then mix well.

2. Cut the rabbits into pieces then rub with the spice mixture.

3. Marinate the spiced rabbits for 3 hours—more time is good but 3 hours is enough.

4.   Preheat a smoker to 225°F (107°C) then place the spiced rabbits in the smoker.

5.   Smoke the rabbits for four hours and when the internal temperature has reached165°F (74°C), remove the smoked rabbits from the smoker.

6.   Place the smoked rabbits on a serving dish then enjoy.

Nutrition:

Carbohydrates: 4g

Protein: 46 g

Fat: 16 g

Sodium: 28 mg

Cholesterol: 95 mg

# 33. The Beer Smoked Rabbit

Preparation time: 30 minutes

Cooking Time: 5 Hours

Servings: 10

Ingredients:

- Rabbits 2 (6-lbs., 2.7-kgs)
- The Rub
- Minced garlic – ¼ cup
- Salt – 2 ½ tablespoons
- The Glaze
- Beer – 3 cups

Directions:

1. Combine salt and minced garlic then rub the rabbits with the mixture. Set aside.

2. Preheat a smoker to 225°F (107°C) with charcoal and hickory wood chips. Prepare indirect smoke.

3. Once the smoker has reached the desired temperature, place the seasoned rabbits in the smoker.

4. Check the smoke and add more wood chips if it is needed.

5. Smoke the rabbit for 3 hours and brush with beer every 15 minutes.

6. Once the rabbits are done, remove from the smoker then check whether the internal temperature has reached 165°F (74°C).

7. Take the rabbits out from the smoker then cut the smoked rabbits into pieces.

8. Transfer to a serving dish then serve.

9. Enjoy!

Nutrition:

Carbohydrates: 4g

Protein: 46 g

Fat: 16 g

Sodium: 28 mg

Cholesterol: 95 mg

# 34. Bacon-Wrapped Little Smokies

Preparation time: 30 minutes

Cooking Time: 6 Hours

Servings: 1

Ingredients:

- 1 lb. of bacon with strips cut into halves
- 14 oz. of cocktail sausages
- ½ cup of brown sugar

Directions:

1.     Take a clean flat surface and lay bacon strips over it

2.     Now use a rolling point and roll them out so that they get an even thickness

3.     Now wrap every sausage in ½ strip of bacon and secure it firmly with a toothpick

4.     Place this wrapped sausages in a casserole dish and cover it with brown sugar

5.     Keep it in the fridge and let it sit for half an hour

6.     When it is ready to cook, fire the grill and set the temperature to 350 degrees F

7.    Now lay these sausages on the parchment-lined cookie sheet and place it on the grill grate

8.    Cook it for almost half an hour until it is crisp

9.    Serve and enjoy

Nutrition:

Carbohydrates: 4g

Protein: 46 g

Fat: 16 g

Sodium: 28 mg

Cholesterol: 95 mg

# 35. Grilled Lemon Pepper Pork Tenderloin

Preparation time: 30 minutes

Cooking Time: 5 Hours

Servings: 1

Ingredients:

- 2 lbs. of pork tenderloin
- 1 clove of minced garlic
- 1 teaspoon of minced fresh parsley
- 1 teaspoon of lemon juice
- ½ teaspoon of kosher salt
- 2 lemon zest
- 2 tablespoon of olive oil
- 1 teaspoon of black pepper

Directions:

1. Take a small bowl and whisk all ingredients except pork tenderloin

2. Now take the tenderloin and trim all the silver skin and get rid of the excess fat

3. Place it in a large zip lock bah

4. Now pour the marinade over the tenderloin and close the zip

5.    Transfer it to the fridge and marinate it for approx. 2 hours

6.    Set the grill to preheat and keep the temperature to 375 degrees F

7.    Remove the tenderloins from the bag and then get rid of the marinade

8.    When the grill has turned hot, put it on the grill grate and then cook for 20 minutes flipping it midway. Make sure the temperature reaches 145 degrees F

9.    Remove from the heat, add sauce and let it rest for approx. 10 minutes

10.   Slice and serve

Nutrition:

Carbohydrates: 4g

Protein: 46 g

Fat: 16 g

Sodium: 28 mg

Cholesterol: 95 mg

# 36. BBQ Baked Beans

Preparation time: 30 minutes

Cooking Time: 7 Hours

Servings: 1

Ingredients:

- 1 lb. of chopped bacon
- 4 cans of pork & beans
- 1 diced green bell pepper
- 1 diced yellow onion
- 1/2 tablespoon onion powder
- 1/2 tablespoon garlic powder
- 1 tablespoon black pepper
- 1/2 tablespoon kosher salt
- 2 tablespoon dry mustard
- 1 cup of ketchup

Directions:

1. Take a sauté pan and place bacon in it over medium heat

2. Cook it thoroughly until the bacon is crisp and the fat has been rendered

3. Strain the excess fat from bacon while keeping 2 tablespoons reserved and then set the bacon aside

4. Keep the reserved fat in the sauté pan and then add pepper along with onion

5. Now sauté it for 10 minutes approx. until the onions turn translucent and the peppers become tender

6. Remove from the heat source and set it aside

7. When it is ready to cook, prepare the grill for preheating and set the temperature to 350 degrees F

8. Take a casserole dish and mix cooked bacon, beans, peppers and onion along with their leftover ingredients. Mix well to combine thoroughly

9. Now cover the casserole with aluminum foil and place it on the grill grate

10. Cook for an hour making sure to stir it occasionally till the sauce has thickened

11. Let it rest for 15 minutes

12. Serve and enjoy

Nutrition:

Carbohydrates: 24g

Protein: 16 g

Fat: 66 g

Sodium: 38 mg

Cholesterol: 95 mg

# 37. Bacon Grilled Cheese Sandwich

Preparation time: 30 minutes

Cooking Time: 4 Hours

Servings: 1

Ingredients:

☐ 1 lb. of cooked apple wood bacon slices; smoked

☐ 9 slices of Texas toast

☐ 16 slices of cheddar cheese

☐ Mayonnaise

☐ Butter

Directions:

1. Set the grill on pre-heat by pushing the temperature to 350 degrees F

2. Now take the bread and lather it with mayonnaise

3. Place 1 piece of cheddar on a slice and then top it with two bacon slices

4. Now, again add another slice of cheese and then seal it with bread

5. Lather butter on the very top of the bread

6. When the grill has turned hot, place the grilled cheese on the grate with the buttered side facing down

7. Now spread butter on the top of the slice facing upwards

8. Cook on this side for 5 to 6 minutes until the grill marks begin to develop and the cheese starts to melt

9. Flip the sandwich and repeat it on the other side

10. Remove from the grill and serve immediately

Nutrition:

Carbohydrates: 24g

Protein: 16 g

Fat: 66 g

Sodium: 38 mg

Cholesterol: 95 mg

# 38. Baked Corn Dog Bites

Preparation time: 30 minutes

Cooking Time: 3 Hours

Servings: 2

Ingredients:

- 15 mini hot dogs
- 1 lightly beaten egg
- 2 cups of all-purpose flour
- 1 cup of milk at room temp
- 1/4 cup of vegetable oil
- 1 tablespoon of dried minced garlic
- 1/2 cup of yellow cornmeal
- 1 teaspoon of baking soda
- 1 tablespoon of coarse salt
- 4 teaspoons of active dry yeast
- 1/4 cup of granulated sugar
- 1/2 teaspoon of cayenne pepper
- 1/2 teaspoon of mustard powder
- Ketchup & mustard for serving

Directions:

1. Set the grill to preheat by keeping the temperature at 375 degrees F

2.    Take a bowl and add yeast along with milk and sugar to it. Keep it aside for 5 minutes

3.    Now, add oil along with salt, mustard powder, all-purpose flour, cayenne pepper, cornmeal, and baking soda. Mix well with a spoon and then knead to make a dough.

4.    Transfer the dough to a bowl and cover it with plastic wrap to keep it aside for 45 minutes

5.    The dough should approximately double in size

6.    Remove the dough from the bowl and then divide it into 15 ounces

7.    Keep it on a surface but make sure first to dust it with flour

8.    Now make use of a rolling pin and roll the dough into 3x3" pieces.

9.    Place the hot dog in the middle of the dough sheet

10.   Roll it thoroughly in the dough and then press the edges to seal it and make 15 corn dog bites

11. Transfer these to a baking pan which is already lined with parchment paper

12. Brush each of them lightly with a beaten egg

13. Sprinkle minced garlic and salt

14. Bake in the smoker for approx. 30 minutes until they turn golden brownish

15. Serve with ketchup or mustard

16. Enjoy

Nutrition:

Carbohydrates: 24g

Protein: 16 g

Fat: 66 g

Sodium: 38 mg

Cholesterol: 95 mg

# 39. Smoked Sausage

Preparation time: 30 minutes

Cooking Time: 6 Hours

Servings: 1

Ingredients:

- ☐ 3 lbs. of ground pork
- ☐ 1 tablespoon of onion powder
- ☐ 1/2 tablespoon ground mustard
- ☐ 1/2 cup of ice water
- ☐ 1 tablespoon of garlic powder
- ☐ 1/2 tablespoon of salt
- ☐ 1 teaspoon of pink curing salt
- ☐ 4 teaspoons of black pepper
- ☐ Hog casings, soaked and rinsed in cold water

Directions:

Take a midsized bowl and combine both the meat and seasonings thoroughly in it

Now add ice water to the meat and mix with your hand making sure everything has been thoroughly mixed

Place this mixture in sausage stuffer and follow the given instructions for seamless operation

Do not overstuff the stuffer or else the casing may burst

When the meat has been stuffed, calculate the desired link length and then twist it a couple of times

Repeat the process for each link

Now set the smoker on pre-heat with the temperature reaching 225 degrees F

Place these links on the grill grate and cook for 2 or 3 hours till the temperature reaches 155 degrees F

Let the sausages rest for some time and then slice

Serve and enjoy

Nutrition:

Carbohydrates: 24g

Protein: 16 g

Fat: 66 g

Sodium: 38 mg

Cholesterol: 95 mg

# 40. Bacon and Sausage Bites

Preparation time: 30 minutes

Cooking Time: 45 minutes

Servings: 4

Ingredients:

- Smoked sausages - 1 pack
- Thick-cut bacon - 1 lb.
- Brown sugar - 2 cups

Directions:

1. Slice ⅓ of the sausages and wrap them around small pieces of sausage. Use a toothpick to secure them.

2. Line a baking tray with baking paper and place the small pieces of wrapped sausage on it.

3. Sprinkle brown sugar on top.

4. Preheat the wood pellet to 300 degrees.

5. Keep the baking tray with the wrapped sausages inside for 30 minutes.

6. Remove and let it stay outside for 15 minutes.

7. Serve warm with a dip of your choice.

Nutrition:

Carbohydrates: 61 g

Protein: 27 g

Fat: 30 g

Sodium: 1384 mg

Cholesterol: 82 mg

# Conclusion

Thank you for making it to the end. The Wood Pellet Smoker Grill will also be an advantage for those who have limited space or are not looking for something that will take up a lot of space. This is because a small wood pellet smoker can be placed on a balcony. It will also allow you to regulate the temperature through the two dampers that can be controlled for both intake and exhaust. It is also an advantage that it takes a minimum amount of time to heat up. This can be anywhere from fifteen to twenty minutes. This is insignificant compared to the time it takes a gas smoker to warm up.

There is almost no chance of ignition when using a wood pellet smoker because it has a controlled ventilation system. The system will automatically help release the heat and replace it with air and empty smoke to maintain the temperature.

When it comes to using the wood pellet smoker, you won't have to seal the lid and coals. This smoker also has an automatic safety feature that when you turn on the unit, you will be reminded with a beep.

You'll also catch a good smell immediately after lighting the wood pellet smoker as the smoke-proof lid is made with chemical paint that will trigger your nose, especially if you have pets or children in the house.

When it comes to choosing your wood pellets, it will be an advantage for you if you have other smokers on hand that you can use for comparison. In general, you will want to choose your wood pellets for the type of food that you want. For example, if you are going to use it for pork, then you will want to have high-quality and good tasting hickory pellets. This type of wood will leave the pork looking and tasting great.

Wood pellet smokers are among the most popular smokers available today. They are among the best smokers is simple. They are also easier to use than other smokers because the intake and exhaust ports are all within easy reach. You will also be able to use the wood pellet smoker at an affordable cost. They also come with many advantages for a variety of indoor and outdoor cooking with great results.

The wood pellets that have been used in the Mythwood pellet smoker that you are now reading that will be a good smoke output. They will produce a heavier smoke, therefore, a better flavor. You will also be using the wood pellets for up to fifteen minutes. This is much better than the time it would take for the smoke to reach its consistency with gas, wood and pellet smokers.

As mentioned, there are many pellet smokers offered by different entities. You will want to make sure that the reviews are good on this product. Of course, you also want to make sure that the cost is under $100. This is to eliminate unnecessary expenses that you may incur for the product.

Wood pellets will more than likely, smell great. Wood pellets will also be a great taste that adds to the flavor of the already great food.

Wood pellets will not leave behind any smoking products used to clean up any mess that will be left in the smoker. You will then be able to cook without having to clean the smoker or worry about where you will be cooking. This is another advantage of wood pellets....

The Mythwood pellet smoker uses red oak ribs and is used for grilling. It also creates a nice glowing briquette that can be used for smoking or grilling indoors or outdoors. These wood pellets can also be lit just on your dime!

The Mythwood pellet smoker doesn't use propane, and you don't need to use lighting, so you'll save money on your electric bills, and you can cook great food and smoke it just as effortlessly.

The Mythwood pellet smoker also has an automatic ignition. This is a safety feature that will keep things from burning if you decide to change the temperature settings without knowing it.

Some of the wood pellets that are available from this unit are kettle wood, lignum, and heartwood. These wood pellets are sold because of their natural essence, and because they offer high smoke production, therefore, burning with wood pellets will not be necessary. You will be able to set a smoke output that will give you an ideal cooking experience.

I hope you have learned something!